I0750277

FINISHING LINE PRESS
www.finishinglinepress.com

I CLOSE MY EYES AND I ALMOST REMEMBER

poems by

Matthew J. Andrews

Finishing Line Press
Georgetown, Kentucky

I CLOSE MY EYES AND I ALMOST REMEMBER

ISBN 978-1-64662-758-5 First Edition

ACKNOWLEDGMENTS

Many thanks to the editors of the publications who first published some of these poems, sometimes in earlier versions and with different titles:

Ancient Paths: "A Toast"
Dodging the Rain: "Three Theories on the Absence of Paul's Wife from Scripture"
Earth & Altar: "Mary Remembers"
inScribe Journal: "The Sixth Day"
Macrina Magazine: "The Cup"
The Penwood Review: "Lord, Teach Us to Pray"
Saint Katherine Review: "Patmos"
Solum Literary Journal: "Peter Goes Fishing on the Sea of Tiberias"
This Present Former Glory: An Anthology of Honest Spiritual Literature: "Isaac at Twilight" and "Hunger"
Time of Singing: "Damascus"

Publisher: Leah Huete de Maines
Editor: Christen Kincaid
Cover Art: Joshua Andrews
Author Photo: Giana Silva, Giana Silva Photography
Cover Design: Elizabeth Maines McCleavy

Order online: www.finishinglinepress.com
also available on amazon.com

Author inquiries and mail orders:
Finishing Line Press
PO Box 1626
Georgetown, Kentucky 40324
USA

Table of Contents

For my wife,
without whom these poems
would not exist

The Sixth Day

In that strange way one can see clearly
only with the gifts of time and distance,

he began to notice he had built his world
to respire, each piece giving up part of its life

to give life to another: the water breathing
out mist to feed clouds, the clouds exhaling

their moisture for the trees, the trees gifting
their richness to the air for the animals,

every breath both generosity and gratitude,
all pulsing together as one beating heart.

Seeing what he had made, this compulsion
come to fruition, he inhaled deeply as he formed

mounds in the dirt with his hands. Then he leaned down,
his face almost touching, and emptied his breath.

Exile

1.

Mostly we walk, rootless wanderings
to nowhere in particular, plodding footsteps

leaving ghostly impressions in the soft dirt,
hours branching into years. We stop

sometimes to rest when we find shade,
sitting with our backs pressed against the trees,

but before long their trunks burn brands
into our skin and we start to retch

with the acrid taste of memory's fruit,
so we lift ourselves up and set off

again, both of us, me beside you,
our arms swinging like clocks out of sync.

2.

I remember when I first bled, that day
we left, when we walked through the briar

patch and the thorn cut a serpentine
pathway across my leg, the blood

running like berries crushed in a fist.
I didn't understand, afraid life

itself was emptying, and you held me
in your arms as we wept and waited

for death. We've since built houses
in the cold climate of our unknowing.

Sometimes at night, while you are sleeping, I drag
a jagged stone over my arm and watch blood

drip into the dirt like raindrops, longing
like a child for that warm embrace.

3.

I miss your eyes, their soft green
like spring buds, the way they got lost

in me back in those early days, back
when we robed ourselves in nakedness.

We are making an existence together, you
and I, planting an orchard, bringing life

where there was once only barren soil,
side by side, each hand as dirty

as the next. But even in moments
where we pretend, where we undress

and make believe all is how it was,
where you give your body to me, all of it,

your eyes are closed, shut tight
like a garden gate, and you can't see me.

Isaac at Twilight

Living in inherited land,
the setting sun

made mountains appear
to him as daggers,

and in the growing darkness,
the begetting pain of memory,

he imagined the cold
clench of steel

in his own fingers,
hovering over the pounding

heartbeat breaths
of his child.

Reflections From Peniel

Scars without
memory
are only
birthmarks.

Without breath,
the sons and daughters
collected at the river's edge
are only stones.

*

Powerless men with a
crippling addiction to divinity,
we sometimes slug it out
on the banks of the river
just to make ourselves
feel alive again.

*

As we walk east,
the bad leg drags,
cutting channels into the dust,
slithering slashes in the earth
like a newly formed stream.

Outstretched Hand

sure,
pharaoh says,
go

balmy sun
settles
on glassy waters

the swelling mass
shuffles silently,
chasing smoke

the staff
discarded
as sawdust

His Glory

After making his desire known, Moses expected flames
on the skyline, for a baptism of oranges and reds
to appear in spontaneous combustion. It was in fire
He had first made Himself known, revealing
the tiniest sliver of His power, so to see the horizon
burn like an ember was no surprise. It was when
the inferno began to engulf the trees, then the people

camped at their feet, then all the land unrolled below
his mountaintop perch, that he began to think
he had underestimated the display of His glory.
And when the heavens began to distort into amoebic
patches of black, expanding perforations of creation undone,
all void and nothingness, he understood how foolish
his petition had been, and how merciless He was in granting it.

Egypt

We are a viscous mass of sap
oozing slowly down a tree.

Do you remember
how we swam naked in the river,
washed by the strength of its current?

Our bodies are rocks, dust-
crumbled, carved by wind.

Do you remember
when we were bronze figures in the sun,
your finger tracing the bulk of my arms?

Slaves to smoke, shackled in fire,
our feet now grind into sand.

Do you remember
how we were once free to sing, holy psalms
dripping like honey from our mouths?

The Prayer of St. Gideon

Please, Lord,

just
one more.
That

will
be enough.

Job's Lecture

Spindly fingers of sunset reach over the horizon
and wrap themselves tightly around my neck,
their heat forming welts on my fragile skin,
air trapped in my mouth like unswallowed fruit.

The creek is a chorus chanting its shrewd refrain;
the waves are war drums pounding the shore.
Before an audience of stars, the grasses ensnare
my ankles, the vines coil around my thin wrists,

the mighty oak's branches force me into the dirt,
and it is here that I am made to listen like a child
to the harsh reprimand of birds pecking my eyes,
to the stern rebuke of lions ripping at my flesh.

Unfinished Psalms From the Private Notebook of King David

I praise you in psalms,
in words I shape from dust,
in songs I form from air.

How much longer until
these praises become worship?

When will they bloom
like flowers in your light?

*

I hear her singing,
her flesh calling to me,
a lone voice at night
like a howling wolf,
like a talking fire,

her skin like olive oil,
her breasts like pomegranates,
her body a ripe fruit
sagging on the branches,
drawing close to my lips.

*

A drunk man collapses on the street—
his face dirty, his robe torn,

the people shamed at his disgrace—
and awakens to gold coins laid out for him.

Such is this crown you have bestowed.

*

I take my baths on the roof,
washing myself in the blood.

I feel her eyes watching,
her seeing my nakedness.

Vulture-priests circle
over the heavy altar.

I will accept no offering
that costs her nothing.

*

Speak to me, please,
in a tone that is not thunder,
in a voice that is not rain.

*

The comfort of wine on the lips,
the warmth of her breast in my mouth;

both liven the blood like fire
but leave ash on the tongue.

*

The swords of my enemies—
Saul, my Lord; Absalom, my son—
plunge into the flesh,
my blood falling like tears.

I am losing perspective,
my nightmares and lusts
forged together into a golden calf.

*

This thorn in my side—
is this your weapon?

This woman in my eye—
is this your accuser?

*

I feel you closest to me
when I am alone in the fields,

in the rolling hills flush with green,
in the grasslands spotted with sheep,

their masses bleating exaltations,
your sky accepting them with joy.

*

This graveyard woman
dances in my court.

Her body is like sunset,
her hips rise like stars

guiding me to my bed.
I am drunk with her lips,

with the condensation of her psalms,
and I follow her into the darkness.

Ezekiel's Wife

Ashen cheeks already as cold
as a winter's morning. Fingers frozen,

pointed down into the dirt.
Hair like spiderwebs. *Is there not*

another way to teach them? Ears
echo with sound but hear nothing.

Eyes sealed like scabs. Tongue
trapped under the rubble of the lips.

Is there not another way
to show them life? The bones, static,

swallowed by Sheol. Rain falling
from the sky but not from my eyes—

prophecy in stoicism. *Is there not*
another man damned to deliver your word?

Mary Remembers

When the dam breaks, the water
                              rushes in to fill the void,
to swallow the emptiness.
                              It is like this with broken lines,
one side overtaking the other:
                              the holy flooding the broken,
history cascading into memory.
                              The ecstasy of conception,
the soft voice of the man of light,
                              the star hovering like a halo—
I feel their truth beating in my heart
                              but see them with crossed eyes
when I look over my shoulder.
                              The cries of the children, their blood
flowing as a river, their crimson
                              coloring those brilliant Egyptian sunsets—
I have heard the story so many times,
                              I close my eyes and I almost remember.

Hunger

If we are a little lower than the angels,
we are not much higher than the beasts:

simple creatures who worship their hungers,
with flesh that lusts for things to be consumed.

I sometimes imagine Jesus in the wilderness,
frail as any man: withering slowly to dust,

the stomach collapsing in ruins, the aromas
of temptation wafting in the lonely desert sky.

How much harder those lingering days
must have been than his climactic one,

when the pain, so acute and overwhelming,
was only temporary, one last obstacle

between the primitive suffering of incarnation
and his return to the waiting arms of glory.

Out there in the empty land, the cross
a lifetime away, subject to the animal

instincts of his creation and the temporal
desires of a human body, a small concession

in exchange for the soft relief of bread
must have sounded like a hell of a deal.

The Gospel According to the Healed Leper

My whole life I have been nothing—
a disfigured accumulation of gnarled bones
and unfinished skin, a discarded façade
of humanity crumpled at the city's gates,

a settling place for the dust of your feet—
so I understand the allure of your heresy,
your belief that just because a holy hand
grazed the skin of my cheek and a voice

of God commanded that I rise, that I am risen
to something worthy of heaven's embrace.
But you miss His point. Yes, I now walk
as you do, and I work, feast, and make love

like I always wanted, but most of me,
the real weight of my soul, still begs
in the dirt, right next to you and the others—
all of us lepers, all of us cripples. How blinded

you are to truth by the coins on your eyes,
by the pedestal platform you've erected—
only someone who has lived as nothing
can see that no one has ever been anything.

Lord, Teach Us to Pray

The Lord built a fire
and sat in weighted silence
as its preaching voice
gradually rose to a roar.

The disciples emulated
as best they could, wordlessly
gazing at the fire, waiting
for something more to come,

until one by one they fell
asleep, leaving only Him
and the flickering flame,
a dancing reflection in His pupils.

Boanerges

To think I used to be so powerless,
just an ordinary man tossing his net
over the side of the boat, waiting
for the world to come to me. Never again.

These days I will grab a man
by his throat and throw him down
so his body smashes like pottery,
his demons dispersing as vapor,

and when my strength is resisted
by faithless dogs who push us aside,
I walk away with pounding footsteps
and manifest gathering clouds

of sulfur, fire welling like rainwater,
smoke hovering as a jurist spirit,
all the while my hands crackling
with lightning: the power and the glory.

The Last Temptation of Judas Iscariot

It
starts as
a whisper, a
softness in the ear,
a silken touch on skin,
a feather sinking, a subtle arousal
settling in the stomach. Then the voice
starts to rise, and in concert, the circulation
throbs with the drumbeat of racing heart, the head
wets with the condensation of want. All rises to fever:
the body overcome with lust and heat, a dark inferno raging
across the flesh, the soul screaming with desire, fixation snuffing out the light.

Last Supper

I dip the bread into the wine
and it limps like a leper's finger

reaching out, begging
for communion with the tongue.

More than anything, I am scared
I will not remember your body,

that I will sit down for a meal
and not know what I am eating,

that my grinding teeth will untether
the two halves of the metaphor.

This softness dissolving in my mouth—
will it be like this when you are gone?

A Toast

Drunk at the bar, Pilate slams his glass
on the table to broadcast his emptiness.
The bartender responds with a wordless pour.

He drinks slowly, aimlessly, trying to ignore
the background noise: the gossip traded
in whispers at the tables, the hushed tears,

the unrestrained gasps of the men gathered
at the window, watching the stretched body
rise and fall in labored breaths, the blood

condensing and dripping like dew in the dirt.
He drinks until the lines between things erode,
until his static body suddenly lurches and rolls,

until the glass slips from his uncommitted fingers
and shatters on the bar. He can only laugh,
so very tired and so very drunk, as he gathers

the shards in a pile, his hands a mixed drink
of blood and wine, and then yells aloud as he
raises them into the air for a toast: *to truth!*

Peter Goes Fishing on the Sea of Tiberias

The fishing is hard with the constant
lapping of rooster crows at the boat,
the trawler weighed down with dredged feathers.

Peter watches the shoreline, thinks about how
the rocks are just sand not yet subjected
to the eroding forces of the wind,

about how the land is just a vacuum
not yet filled by water. On the beach
there is a fire burning with smoke

signals rising in pillars, a man
crouched beside it, the morning sun
reflecting off the sword at his side.

Peter knows the man, has always
known the man, as if the moth
could ever forget the call of the flame.

He steps over the side, places the weight
of his feet on the water, and walks to shore,
buoyant, weightless. The sword unsheathes

and summons by name. He closes his eyes,
feels the steel at his neck, determined,
for once, to be faithful to something.

Damascus

The truth is, anyone can listen to thunder,
to that deep ancestral growl that tremors
under the skin after the luminous knife blade

has cut across the sky and left you in darkness.
Any man can hear the proclamations of fire
consuming the forests, can read the charges

of heaven crackling in the electric sky. Fewer
are those who heed the quiet teaching of rain
as it softly patters against the roof, as it seeps

slowly under the door frame and forms pools
at your feet, as it trickles down your face
and onto your fingers, one small drop at a time.

Three Theories on the Absence of Paul's Wife from Scripture

1.

She was as diminutive as Paul demanded,
filling his cup with tea as he wrote furiously
and then stepping back, hands folded, silent,
always silent, always tending, until she faded
hoarsely into mist, even her name forgotten.

2.

She saw the same light as Paul, fell face down
into the same dirt, but she kept her eyes
and watched the terrible flames of heaven
engulf the Lord's voice, and she instead chose
to scurry as a cockroach back into the darkness.

3.

Paul loved her with such immensity that in embrace
he felt her thorn dig deep down into his flesh,
and after he swam for shore on the Lord's
business, leaving her as flotsam in the wreckage,
he couldn't again bring her name to his lips.

The Calling of Onesimus

There are nightmares most nights: whipcrack
voices and the iron glowing like magma.

The Lord often speaks to us in fire,
the old man is fond of saying.
I visit him each week, him in chains,
writing letters as a guard hovers.
I am a prisoner of my God, he preaches.
You do His work and are yet punished,
I say, You sound like His slave.
He laughs: *Yes. I am that too.*

Sometimes I feel the cane thumping
against my body and wake up bruised.

I do not want to go back, I confess.
You must do as you are commanded,
he responds, *You are no longer your own.*
I remind him I have never once been my own.

The darkness is constricting: the swallowing
walls, the hands gripped tight around the neck.

It will be different this time, he says.
I am worth nothing, I tell him,
It is possible that he will kill me.
Then a blessed death worthy of life,
he concludes before sending me away.

I watch the evening sun fade to stars
through my window, fighting with every breath
against the inevitable entrapment of sleep.

Patmos

It is here, under the heavy blanket of silence
that accompanies exile, with the body cut

in patterns by the skin wrinkled with age,
that he finally understands how one can be

surrounded by life, in a garden of ancient trees swaying
in the wind and flowers opening themselves

to the beckoning of sun, and be so empty.
How one can look up at the star-speckled

heavens and see the shapes of prowling beasts,
each floodlit by the fire on the horizon.

How one can stack stones into temples,
blood on the brow, eyes red with grief,

and imagine what it is to be reborn
to give birth to something new.

The Cup

With the sky still draped in black, the son,
dazed by the fog-shroud of sleep,
is roused to wake by the father and his stern

command: *Get up. It's time to go.*
The son rises, dresses slowly in the dark,
and walks solemnly through the moonlit

halls of the empty mansion. In the armory,
he wordlessly sharpens swords and shines them
with shaky hands so each is an unblemished

mirror. In the stable, the horses fidget
in agitation, but the son strokes their manes
and whispers soothing songs to calm

their collective nerves. At the cusp
of dawn, he mounts his steed and looks east,
where the fire of day will soon ignite,

leaving a world of ashes in its wake.
He sighs deeply and prays as he sets off:
yet not my will, but yours be done.

The Gardener

Everything now washed and cleaned, hands
scrubbed of grime and napkins neatly folded
in laps, the man dines with his children

at a table overflowing with platters of roasted birds,
mashed potatoes with rich gravy, and spiced lamb,
baskets of bread, endless wine, conversation

that meanders like a walk in the forest. And he
is happy, happier than he has been in a long time,
to see this heaping table, this house of laughter,

this assembly of prodigal children returned.
Yet as the meal goes on, each empty plate
replaced with a full one, he finds himself

looking out the window and into the void erased
of light, that cold black emptiness abandoned,
and imagining that it looks a lot like dirt,

the kind he used to scoop into his weathered fingers
and let fall like rain, and with a smile he
thinks to himself: *I should plant myself a garden.*

Notes on the Poems

"The Sixth Day" is inspired by Genesis 1-2.

"Exile" is inspired by Genesis 3.

"Isaac at Twilight" is inspired by Genesis 22.

"Reflections From Peniel" is inspired by Genesis 32.

"Outstretched Hand," "His Glory," and "Egypt" are inspired by the book of Exodus. "His Glory" is further inspired by an untitled piece from Patty Paine's collection of damaged photo negatives: https://www.instagram.com/p/B8rT2CRHazk/.

"The Prayer of St. Gideon" is inspired by Judges 6.

"Job's Lecture" in inspired by Job 38-41.

"Unfinished Psalms From the Private Notebook of King David" is inspired by the book of Psalms and the various books detailing the life of King David.

"Ezekiel's Wife" is inspired by Ezekiel 24.

"Mary Remembers" is inspired by Matthew 1-2 and is heavily indebted to the writings of Marcus Borg.

"Hunger" is inspired by the temptation of Jesus in the Gospels of Matthew, Mark, and Luke.

"The Gospel According to the Healed Leper" is generally inspired by the healing stories in the four Gospels.

"Lord, Teach Us to Pray" is a conglomeration of images and inspirations from the four Gospels.

"Boanerges" is inspired by Luke 9.

"The Last Temptation of Judas Iscariot," "Last Supper," "A Toast," and "Peter Goes Fishing on the Sea of Tiberias" are all generally inspired by the narrative of Jesus' death and resurrection in the four Gospels.

"Damascus" is inspired by Acts 9.

"Three Theories on the Absence of Paul's Wife From Scripture" is generally inspired by the writings on and of Paul in various books.

"The Calling of Onesimus" is inspired by Philemon.

"Patmos," "The Cup," and "The Gardener" are inspired by Revelation.

Matthew J. Andrews is a writer who lives in Modesto, California. He graduated with a B.A. in English from California State University, Stanislaus, but it was more than a decade before he discovered his love for poetry and began writing it in earnest. Since then, his poetry has appeared in numerous literary journals, including *EcoTheo, Orange Blossom Review, ONE ART, St. Katherine Review, Kissing Dynamite, Sojourners, Funicular Magazine,* and *Presence: A Journal of Catholic Poetry*, among others. He also serves as an Assistant Poetry Editor at Solum Literary Press. *I Close My Eyes and I Almost Remember* is Matthew's first collection.

When he is not writing, Matthew is a professional private investigator, a voracious reader, an amateur chef, a wannabe outdoorsman, a sometimes runner, a doting husband, and a competent father of two.

More information about Matthew can be found at matthewjandrews.com.

www.ingramcontent.com/pod-product-compliance
Lightning Source LLC
LaVergne TN
LVHW051022080826
845145LV00009B/2760